Musings
Philip J. Tate

Philip J. Tate

Musings

Published by Spines Publishing Platform

Isbn: 979-8-89691-667-3

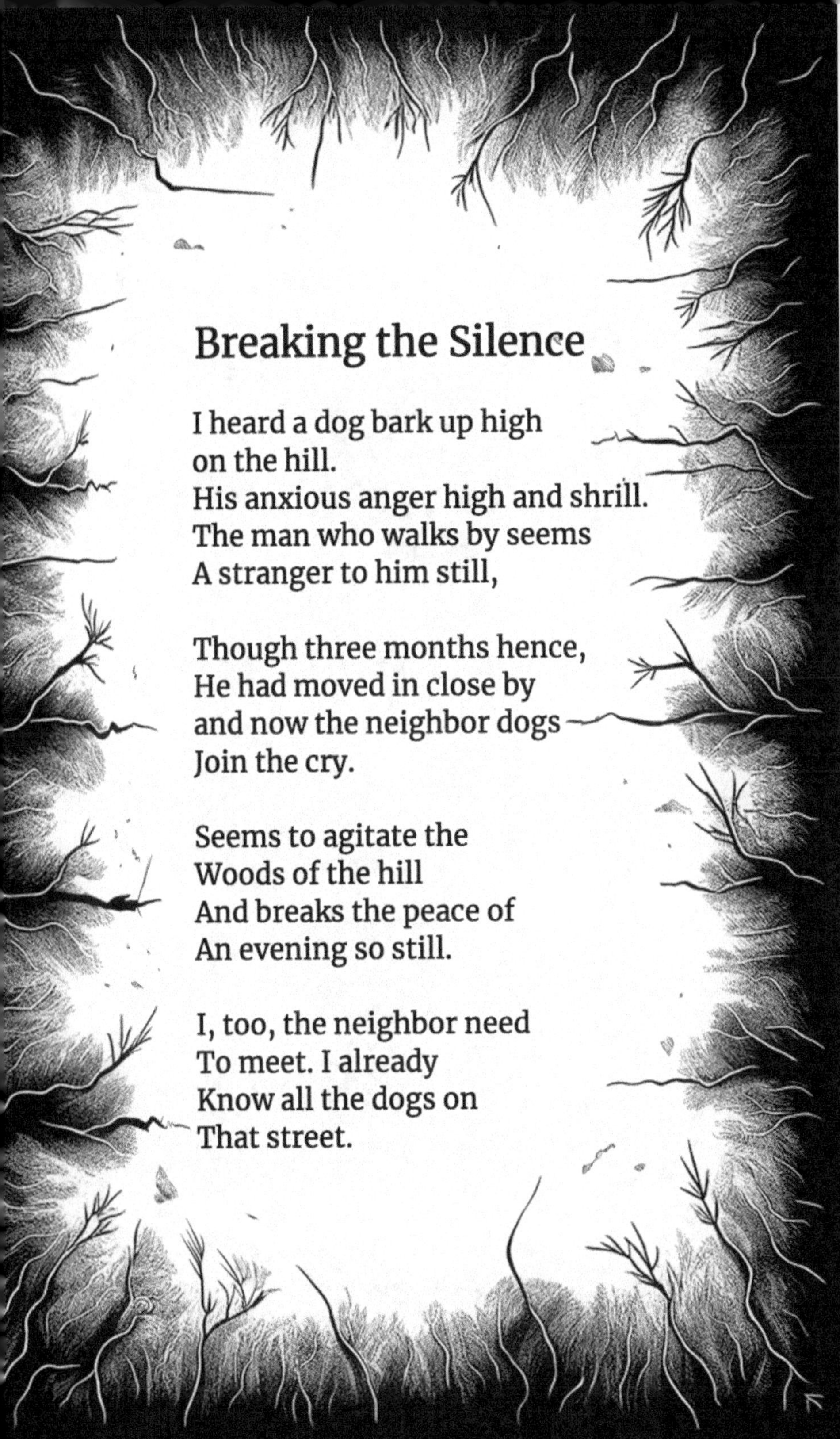

Breaking the Silence

I heard a dog bark up high
on the hill.
His anxious anger high and shrill.
The man who walks by seems
A stranger to him still,

Though three months hence,
He had moved in close by
and now the neighbor dogs
Join the cry.

Seems to agitate the
Woods of the hill
And breaks the peace of
An evening so still.

I, too, the neighbor need
To meet. I already
Know all the dogs on
That street.

Cast Off Valor

On that field of conflict
I was kicking around
In the leaves of
That ground, that had borne a
battle of long ago.

And stubbed up an artifact
With my toe.

Rusty as it was, I uncovered it – a
bayonet replete.

Whose it was I did not
Know and whether he had
Fallen on blood-stained
Snow.

To a child like me what
A treasure to find
A trophy of a time
When armies were unkind.

No mercy given within the
Ire of men and weapons
Clashing fire.

Where fear and courage
Live one and same.

The ground receives
The remnants and
The reasons and the
Tools of the game.

Hot Reel

It came out like a rocket
At least I thought to see.

It was a fish but a rocket
It looked to me.

To my best friend, whose reel
Did sing, a most exciting
Fight this Wahoo fish would
bring.

To be on the ocean that
Glorious fine day

My friend, the watching of
His fish to play.

Was as joyous a thing
For a man could pray.

On Point

She was a setter dog
And a pet to boot!

She's run all day
For quail to shoot.

And when she smelled
That covey sly,

She froze in point
Least they would fly.

For master's hunt
Her work prevail.

To see and find
The crafty quail.

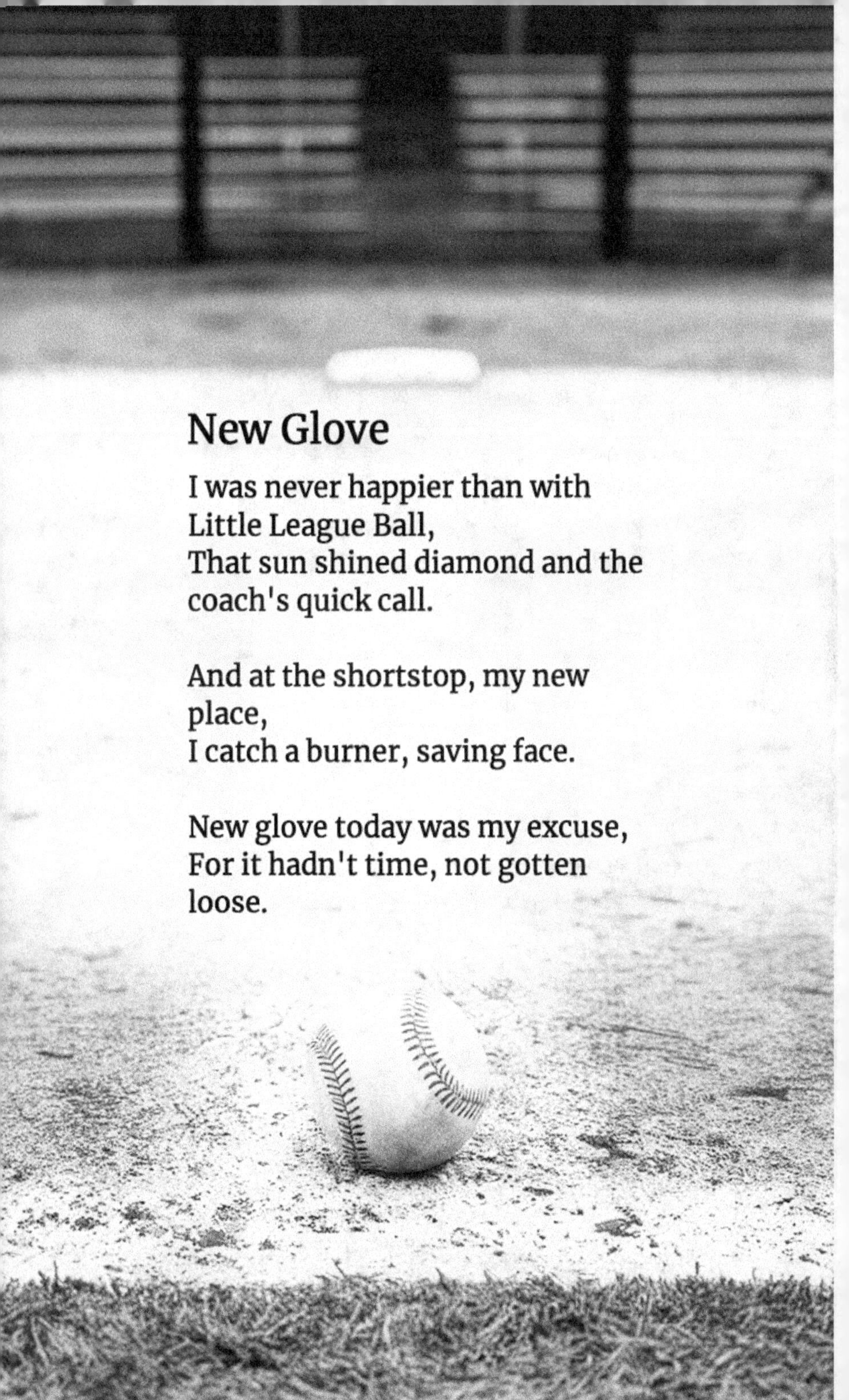

New Glove

I was never happier than with
Little League Ball,
That sun shined diamond and the
coach's quick call.

And at the shortstop, my new
place,
I catch a burner, saving face.

New glove today was my excuse,
For it hadn't time, not gotten
loose.

Treasure

To find some change in an old
jean's pocket,
With which to buy my girlfriend's
locket
Was a treasure trove born by
happy hand.

To the jewelry store with avid
heart
To gift her in hopes it'd be a start.

The locket wasn't much as
glamorous
As the hopeful suitor, much too
amorous.

The Plight

Don't send me off to war without
a solid reason.
Don't say that this, too, as all
things has its season.

For to send me in no truth to tell
Is sending a soul into wicked hell.

Kite Flying

March is windy fine for kite flying.
And on the hill back the house
A perfect sky way for long kite exploration

The hill so high as to catch the wind
No trees to impede the sticks and paper send.

An aircraft tethered by a string.

To Short off, miles away, the river or the moon.

Mobile

132 spokes turning and an old black cat
Eating road out Memphis way, running like a bat
Out of... Hello. Operator, can you give me #9?

My chain's a little loose but her engine's running fine.

Ol' cat with helmet rides my back with claws dug in
like a rattlesnake attack.

We ride back roads toward Memphis as the sun goes down.

The gutted mufflers rumbling till we finally do hit town.

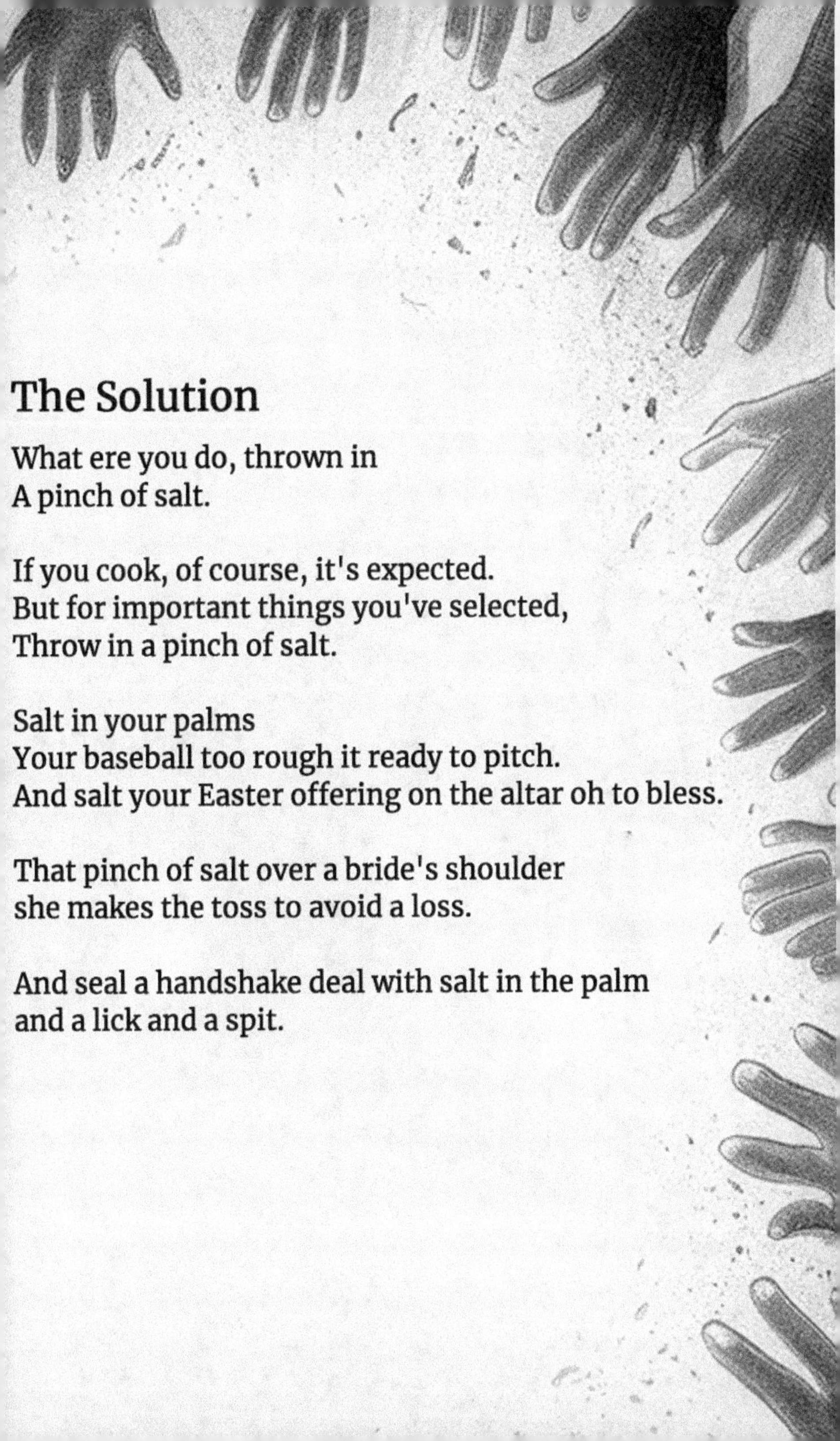

The Solution

What ere you do, thrown in
A pinch of salt.

If you cook, of course, it's expected.
But for important things you've selected,
Throw in a pinch of salt.

Salt in your palms
Your baseball too rough it ready to pitch.
And salt your Easter offering on the altar oh to bless.

That pinch of salt over a bride's shoulder
she makes the toss to avoid a loss.

And seal a handshake deal with salt in the palm
and a lick and a spit.

I Saw Them Coming

My name is Zebulon.
I am a horneytoad living at the foot of Mt. Sinai.

And I first saw a tall fiery cloud in the sky —
afar off yet headed our way.

It was glorious.

Then, I saw the dust cloud.

That night I saw the cloud of fire and the campfires.

After two days, I felt the vibrations of 600,000 at my
underbelly as the Earth shook.

The trembling got greater.

It was Moses and the Hebrews now freed.

I was a witness at Sinai.

Zebulon Horneytoad.

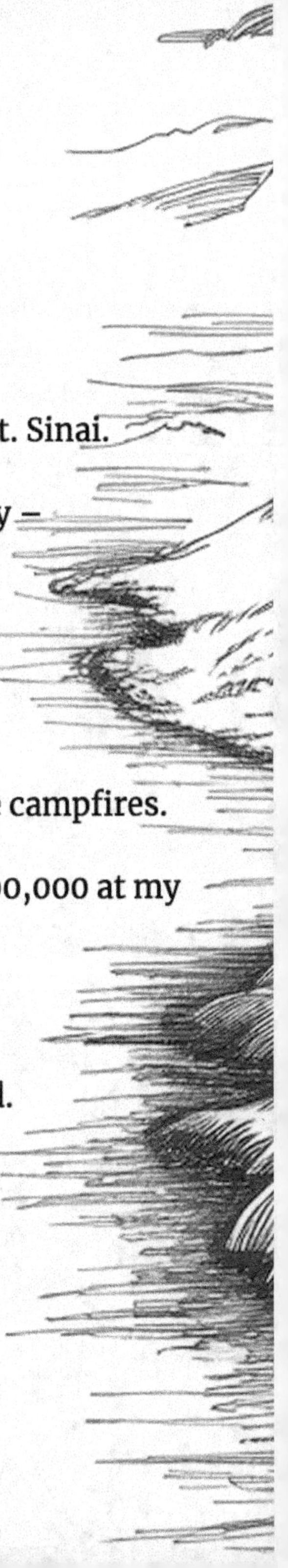

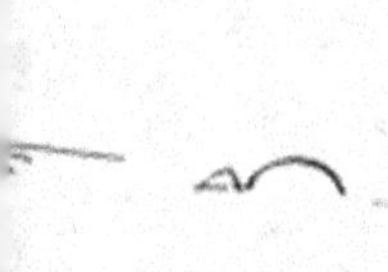

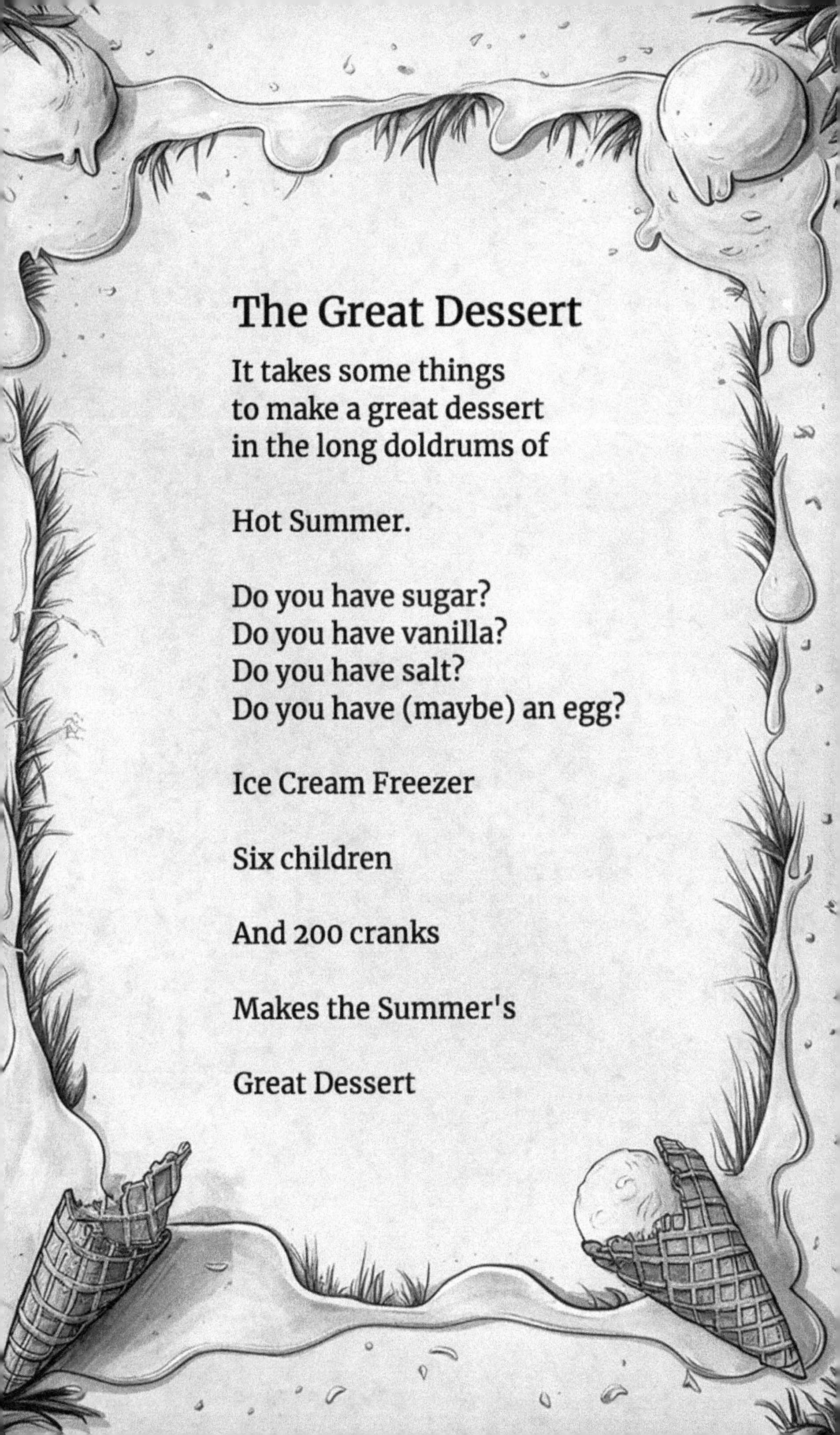

The Great Dessert

It takes some things
to make a great dessert
in the long doldrums of

Hot Summer.

Do you have sugar?
Do you have vanilla?
Do you have salt?
Do you have (maybe) an egg?

Ice Cream Freezer

Six children

And 200 cranks

Makes the Summer's

Great Dessert

Cool Phrase But Dated

My friend Joe used to always say it.
The jukebox used to always play it.

With pancakes, you always have to use it.

Sometimes it takes a coin to call it.

Flip side

"See you on the flip side."

Company

There's a place where I arrive that there comes company.
They call and light in a nearby tree and look at me.
And I click at them and they call back
With a Caw, Caw! Caw, Caw!

This has happened with as many as five in a tree by me.

Hence, my name has become Samuel Crow Talker
when I'm with them.
And to me, when I'm not.

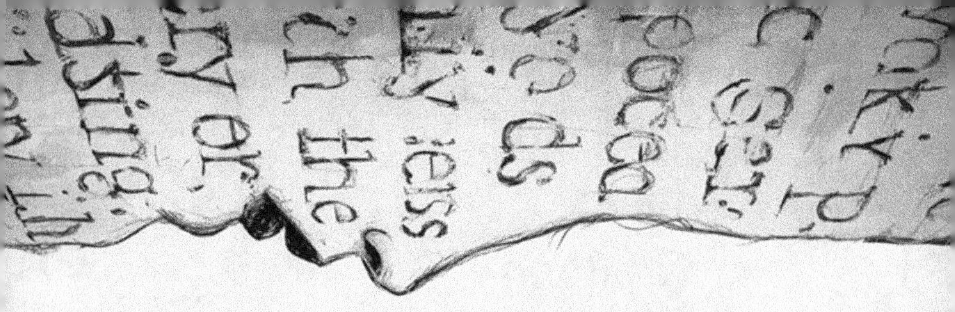

Freshman Poison

It was a dorm mixer at the University, you see,
And it had co-eds which helped the dim view of the
darkened place.

And it was crowded and they were doling out
Horrible gin.

But there was a raven dark-haired beauty
And she was from Gastonia
And she was drop dead gorgeous
And like Scarlett O'Hara's suitors gathered

Yet she was not looking for a Freshman that night.
Experienced she was and for her only a Senior would do.

They were men with Cars!

No Bond

The woman came and showed
Her shame for the bonds–
Man would refuse her.

Guardian appointed she was
And needed a court bond
For she was guardian
Of her mother.

Yet in her report
She would retort that
She charged her mother
For every little thing

A drive
to the Dr.
or groceries
or even church.

Irate, the bondsman ordered her away.

"No Love, No bond,"
He said without pause.

Bakery

Two six-year-olds were passing notes
over time:

I love you. Do you love Me?

And the teacher would catch them

And everyone would laugh.

But after school,
They would meet at the bakery
and share a doughnut.

6-year unrequited Love

The Pot Lid

It was a formation of nature
Made of pine trees on a hill
Forming a pot lid shape.

And the pines were tall and very dense.

This was a magical, but formidable place.

First, it was a hunters' landmark
Everyone knew where the pot lid was.

And the crows roosted there. Hundreds.

And we would seek to bushwhack them
in the evenings
As they came home to roost.

Yet they had a job
And it made us leave at dusky dark,
For there were sunken slave graves strewn
through the woods under the tall trees
That the crows guarded at night.

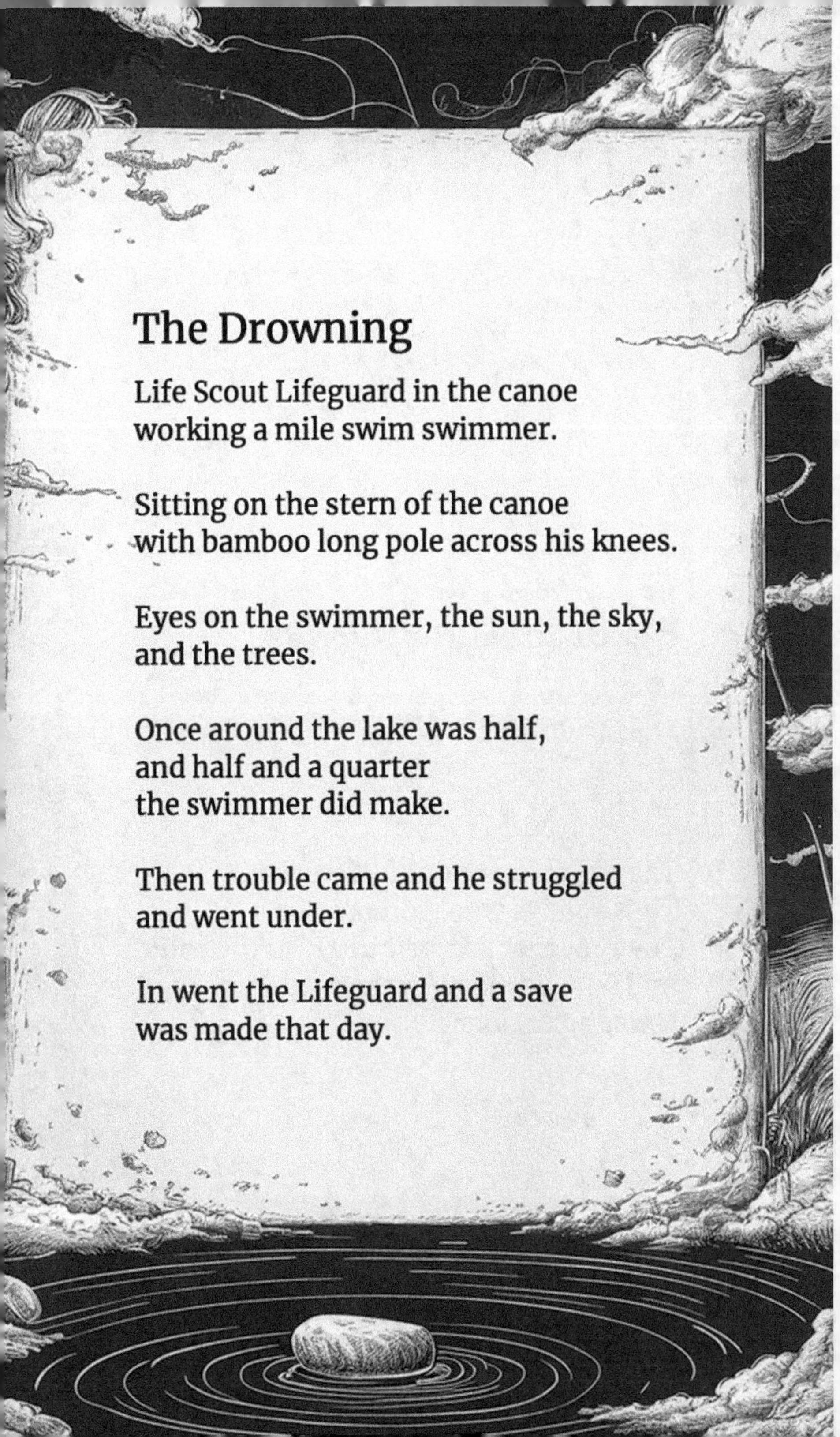

The Drowning

Life Scout Lifeguard in the canoe
working a mile swim swimmer.

Sitting on the stern of the canoe
with bamboo long pole across his knees.

Eyes on the swimmer, the sun, the sky,
and the trees.

Once around the lake was half,
and half and a quarter
the swimmer did make.

Then trouble came and he struggled
and went under.

In went the Lifeguard and a save
was made that day.

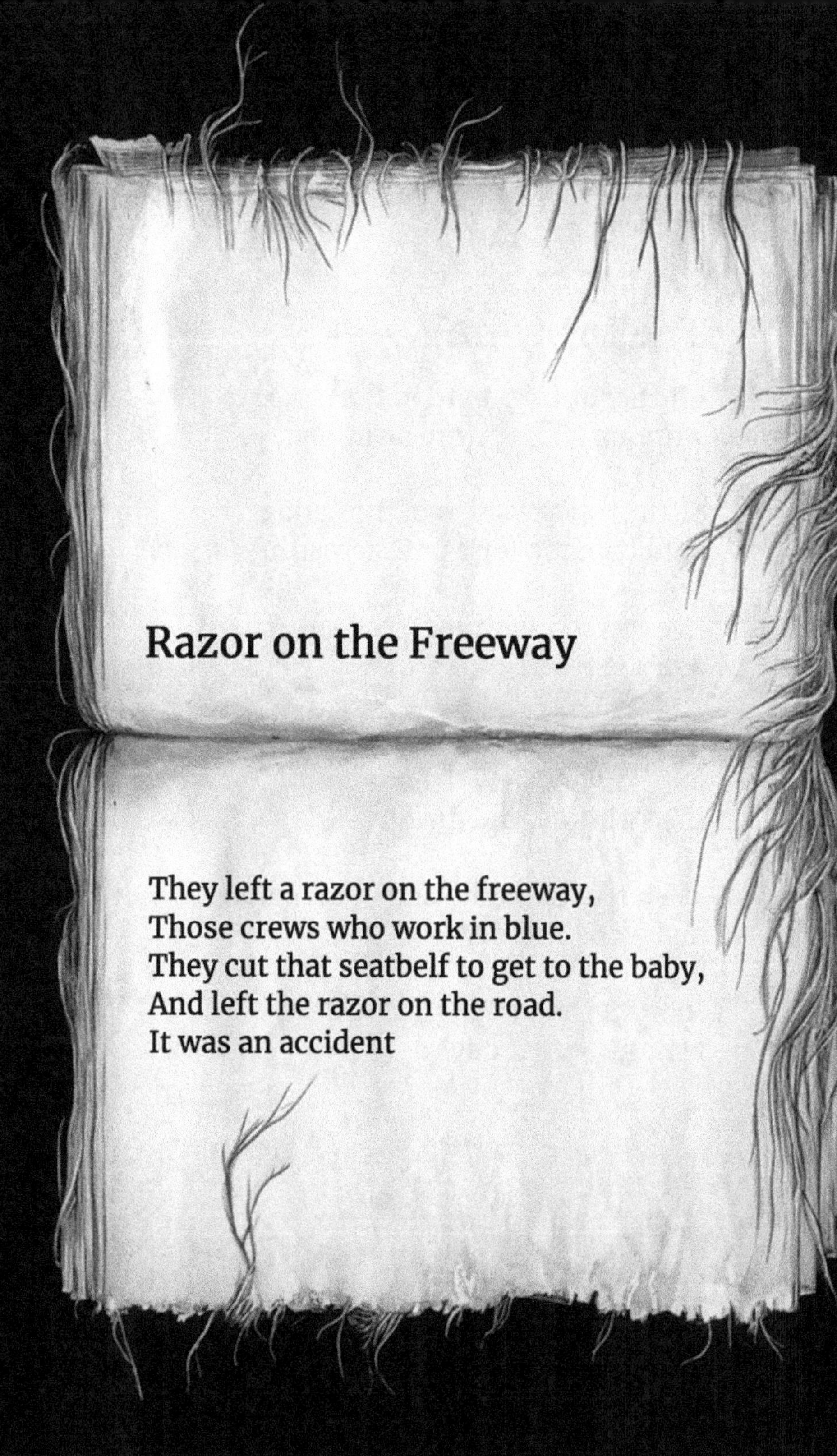

Razor on the Freeway

They left a razor on the freeway,
Those crews who work in blue.
They cut that seatbelf to get to the baby,
And left the razor on the road.
It was an accident

Sitting on the Dock of the Bay

Babysitting is a pensive thing.
Water Bay.
Bay Rum cologne or to drink ready for a date
Or to be held at bay
On the date,
Or for to drink
Or on the dock

"Who's the Baysayer, they say/"

It's a pensive thing.

www.ingramcontent.com/pod-product-compliance
Lightning Source LLC
Chambersburg PA
CBHW051338150726
47997CB00004B/1518